The Zuni

KEVIN CUNNINGHAM
AND PETER BENOIT

Children's Press®
An Imprint of Scholastic Inc.
New York   Toronto   London   Auckland   Sydney
Mexico City   New Delhi   Hong Kong
Danbury, Connecticut

Content Consultant
Scott Manning Stevens, PhD
Director, McNickle Center
Newberry Library
Chicago, Illinois

Library of Congress Cataloging-in-Publication Data

Cunningham, Kevin, 1966–
  The Zuni/Kevin Cunningham and Peter Benoit.
    p. cm. — (A true book)
  Includes bibliographical references and index.
  ISBN-13: 978-0-531-20761-1 (lib. bdg.)   978-0-531-29303-4 (pbk.)
  ISBN-10: 0-531-20761-7 (lib. bdg.)   0-531-29303-3 (pbk.)
1. Zuni Indians—Juvenile literature. I. Benoit, Peter, 1955– II. Title.
  E99.Z9C86 2011
  978.9004'97994—dc22   2010050846

All rights reserved. Published in 2011 by Children's Press, an imprint of Scholastic Inc.
Printed in China 62
SCHOLASTIC, CHILDREN'S PRESS, A TRUE BOOK and associated logos are trademarks and/or registered trademarks of Scholastic Inc.

1 2 3 4 5 6 7 8 9 10 R 19 18 17 16 15 14 13 12 11

Find the Truth!

Everything you are about to read is true *except* for one of the sentences on this page.

Which one is **TRUE**?

T or F The Zuni used rock carvings to help guide them to water.

T or F The Zuni did not participate in the Pueblo Revolt of 1680.

Find the answers in this book.

Owl-shaped pottery created by a Zuni craftsperson

Contents

THE **BIG** TRUTH!

Zuni dancer

Prayer stick

4 Zuni Beliefs

What gods and spirits are part of the
Zuni religion? **33**

5 The Zuni Today

What are some of the problems
Zuni face today? **41**

Pottery making is
one of the oldest
Zuni crafts.

5

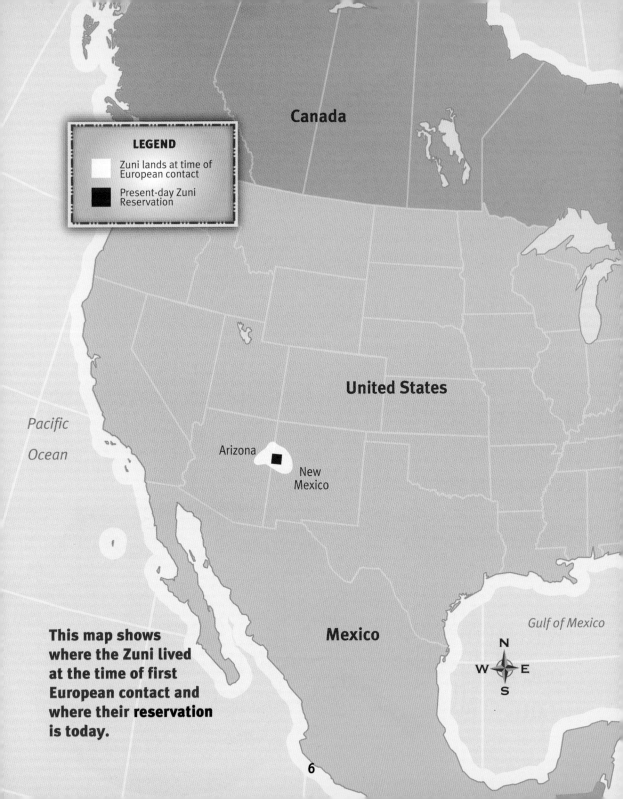

LEGEND

- Zuni lands at time of European contact
- Present-day Zuni Reservation

Canada

United States

Pacific Ocean

Arizona

New Mexico

Mexico

Gulf of Mexico

This map shows where the Zuni lived at the time of first European contact and where their reservation is today.

N
W E
S

CHAPTER 1

A People Like No Other

Travel about 35 miles (56 kilometers) south of Gallup, New Mexico, and you enter another world— the land of the Zuni. The Zuni belong to a group of Native American peoples known as the Pueblo. The Pueblo grew out of a number of ancient peoples who lived more than 1,000 years ago in what is today the southwestern United States.

The Zuni also call themselves the Ashiwi.

In some ways, modern Zuni live as their ancestors did. Old-style **adobe** dwellings, for example, still stand alongside modern houses built from concrete blocks. Unlike many native peoples, most Zuni still speak their own language. Their language, also called Zuni, is unique. It is not related to any other language, which makes it very hard to learn unless a speaker grows up hearing it. Many Zuni, however, can and do speak English to non-Zuni.

A mix of traditional and modern buildings can be found at Zuni Pueblo, which is home to roughly 10,000 Zuni.

Prayer sticks are offered at certain Zuni religious events. They are meant to please the spirits and grab their attention.

After prayer stick offerings, the giver must avoid quarreling with others for a set number of days.

Holding On to Religion

The Zuni are one of the few native peoples to follow the same religion as their ancestors. Spanish officials tried to force them to follow the Catholic faith. But the Zuni resisted. Today, Zuni religion continues to be part of daily life. For instance, Zuni artists pray to the Earth Mother before digging clay for pottery.

Today, visitors are awed by the small city that the Ancient Pueblo constructed beneath a rock ledge at Mesa Verde.

Zuni History

The Ancient Pueblo were the ancestors of the Zuni as well as most of the Pueblo Indians. They built some of the most spectacular Native American towns in North America. Thanks to their skill and the dry climate, the buildings have lasted into modern times. Today, thousands of people visit Ancient Pueblo ruins at Mesa Verde, Colorado, and Chaco Canyon, New Mexico, every year. Some sites have complexes with dozens and even hundreds of rooms.

This Ancient Pueblo dwelling contains 151 rooms.

Pueblo del Arroyo, located in Chaco Canyon, was abandoned more than 900 years ago.

As the towns grew, the people living there built roads, grew crops, and made gorgeous pottery. Then, in the 1100s, they began to leave the towns. By the mid-1200s, the buildings had been closed up and left behind. Why did the people leave? Some experts in **archaeology** think the climate became too dry to grow food. Others believe that war forced the Ancient Pueblos to find safer homes. Some of those people became the Zuni.

Coronado went broke looking for Cíbola.

Francisco Vásquez de Coronado

Contact With the Spanish

The Spanish began to explore the Americas soon after Christopher Columbus arrived in 1492. In 1539, the Spanish explorer Francisco Vásquez de Coronado sent a group of men into what would become New Mexico. A brief fight in the Zuni village of Hawikuh drove the Spanish away. But they would be back. One of the Spaniards told Coronado the Zuni villages were the **mythical** Seven Cities of Gold, called Cíbola.

Coronado soon came to see for himself. But instead of golden cities, he found about 3,000 Zuni living in seven small villages. Their buildings were built out of stones cemented together by adobe—a mixture of sand, clay, water, and straw. After a battle, the Zuni in one village fled safely to the top of a nearby **mesa**. Coronado defeated the others but only remained a short time.

Although Coronado never found the Seven Cities of Gold, the Spanish would eventually create settlements in lands he explored.

This church is considered one of the best examples of Spanish architecture in New Mexico.

The Spanish established churches at Zuni villages in an effort to spread Christianity.

Religion and Raiders

By 1610, Spanish settlers had named the region New Mexico. As the Spanish took over, the Zuni faced serious threats to their culture. Spanish landowners, for example, made the Zuni work to provide them with food. In return, the Spanish were supposed to protect the Zuni. But many landowners turned the Zuni into slaves. At the same time, the Catholic church tried to force the Zuni away from their religious **traditions** and toward being Catholic.

As time passed, the Zuni faced more pressures. **Drought** killed their crops. European diseases hit the people hard. Two other native peoples, the Navajo and the Apache, began to raid Zuni villages. As the drought worsened and the Spaniards failed to protect them, the Zuni lost respect for Spanish ideas. Soon, they returned to their traditional religion. Furious Catholic officials burned the masks and **sacred** dolls that the Zuni used in their religious **rituals**. That, in turn, angered the Zuni.

The word *Apache* is taken from the Zuni word for "enemy."

Corn Mountain is 500 feet (150 meters) high.

In 1680, the Zuni fled to the top of Corn Mountain, where they lived in a village for 12 years.

The Zuni Fight Back

In 1680, the Zuni joined most of the other Pueblo peoples and attacked the Spanish settlers. The Spaniards retreated to Santa Fe, their main city. Eventually, the Spanish ran out of water and left. The Pueblo peoples had won. But without Spanish soldiers around, the Navajo and Apache horsemen raided even more. The Zuni moved to the top of Corn Mountain, a nearby mesa. There they could more easily fight off their enemies.

Breathing Room

The Spanish returned to New Mexico in 1692. The Zuni and other Pueblo peoples united in their fight against the Spanish. Violence between the Zuni and the Spanish continued on and off for a few years. The Spanish, however, saw that it would be too difficult to make the Zuni give up their traditions. Catholic officials tried to ignore the Zuni rituals. The landowners also eased their harsh treatment of workers. The Zuni had earned enough respect to save their religion and way of life.

After the Spanish returned to New Mexico in 1692, they allowed the Pueblo peoples to observe their traditional religious practices and ceremonies.

Zuni Firefighters

Starting in 1951, the U.S. Forest Service and other government agencies teamed up to train a group of Zuni firefighters. Soon the Zuni Thunderbirds had a reputation for handling the worst wildfires. Because they were in such demand, they sometimes worked without helmets and proper firefighting gear. Zunis helped save countless trees across the West—just as they have done for centuries on their own lands. Today, more than 5,000 people from many American Indian nations battle fires.

A Zuni firefighter dumps soil onto a burning log.

These cliff dwellings were built by the Sinagua people, who disappeared without a trace in the 1300s.

CHAPTER 3

Kivas and Carvings

Life in the dry, high-altitude regions of New Mexico shaped Zuni ways and culture. The Zuni's ancestors, for example, built their first houses in the openings of cliffs in the area. But they could not use a lot of wood for buildings. The forests in the Zuni homeland often grew far from the villages, and early Zuni lacked the wheel and large animals to pull logs. Sandstone and the ingredients for adobe, however, were all around.

The Sinagua were ancestors of the Zuni and Hopi peoples.

Nearly 40 kivas have been identified at Pueblo Bonito.

Pueblo Bonito was an Ancient Pueblo village. The Ancient Pueblo are culturally related to the Zuni.

The Kiva

The Zuni continued the Ancient Pueblo peoples' tradition of building pueblos, or villages. In addition to having places to live, a pueblo contained open public squares and important underground rooms called **kivas**. In large kivas, four wooden or stone pillars held up the roof. Most kivas were round, though today many are square. A round kiva at the ancient Pueblo Bonito in Chaco Canyon was more than 60 feet (18 m) wide.

A fire pit inside the kiva played an important part in kiva ceremonies. Smoke rose out of the kiva through a hole in the roof. The Zuni also created a hole, called a *sipapu,* that represented a door they used to pass from their old world to this one. A kiva was only for males. To enter, men and boys climbed down a ladder, because a kiva had no doors.

A ladder descends into an Ancient Pueblo kiva. Some Zuni kivas are similar to those of the Ancient Pueblo.

Joining a Kiva

When a boy is born, his parents select which kiva he will join. As he grows up, older kiva members teach and test him. In this way, the kiva society passes on the traditions of the Zuni's ancestors. The Zuni also group into societies of healers and priests, who have the important job of praying for rain. These societies, unlike a kiva, allow both males and females.

Pictured is a group of Zuni boys and young men in 1873. Although parents chose a kiva for their son, he could choose to join a different one.

If a Zuni couple divorced, their children remained with the mother.

Zuni children were cherished members of the clan.

Clans

Clans, or large family groups, played an important role in Zuni life. For example, in some cases only members of a certain clan could become priests. In Zuni tradition, a married man went to live with his wife's clan. Their children then became attached to the mother's family. Zuni mothers also passed property to their daughters rather than their sons.

Growing the Three Sisters

Even though the land was dry, the Zuni managed to grow what Native Americans called the Three Sisters: maize (corn), beans, and squash. To do this, Zuni farmers trapped melted snow and rainwater with dams. Then they used the pools to **irrigate**, or water, their crops. Long droughts, however, sometimes ruined Zuni plans. They accepted that drought might drive a village to move to a place with more water.

The Zuni were excellent farmers. A Zuni family is shown here planting crops.

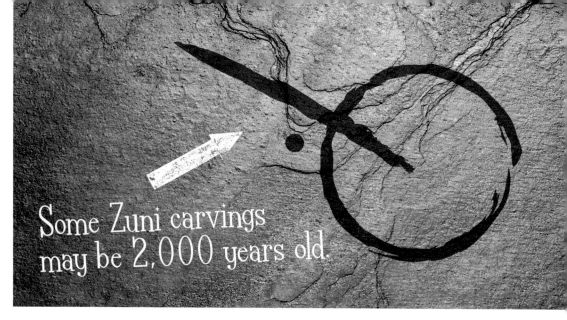

Some Zuni carvings may be 2,000 years old.

Many of the Zuni rock carvings are similar to the one shown here.

Water This Way

The Zuni's need for water may be the answer to an archaeological mystery. For years, archaeologists exploring a 2,000-square-mile (5,200 sq km) region along the Utah-Arizona-Nevada borders have found shapes carved into rock. At first, they did not understand the meaning of the strange symbols. But research suggests the Zuni and neighboring peoples may have used the carvings as signs to lead the way to water sources.

Zuni Farming Life

Zuni men tended the large fields that grew the Three Sisters. Women worked to grow other plants in smaller square gardens surrounded by walls. Their ability to get the most out of land close to home gave the Zuni a reputation as excellent farmers. Irrigation had limits, however. The Zuni then turned to other ways of getting food. They hunted for meat and gathered hundreds of wild plants.

Gardens

Smaller gardens were used to grow plants such as onions, melons, and pumpkins. Walls surrounding each garden protected the plants from wind and hot temperatures.

Valuable Bird

The Zuni kept flocks of turkeys. However, the Zuni only ate the birds in an emergency. Instead, they raised turkeys for feathers that went into clothes or were used during special religious rituals.

Sheep

The Spanish brought sheep to the Southwest. Soon after, the Zuni added sheep ranching to their farming skills. They raised the animals for wool and sold lambs to earn money to buy Spanish goods.

Zuni Art

The Ancient Pueblo peoples made baskets and pottery. Today, pottery made by the Ancient Pueblo are valuable Native American **artifacts**. But the potters then were usually not interested in art. A

A Zuni woman weaves a basket.

pot had an everyday purpose—to carry water or store food. The Zuni continued the ancient basket-making and pottery traditions. They made pots from clay dug out of the ground near their homes. Paints came from plants.

The Zuni liked to decorate everyday pots with sunflowers and white-tailed deer. The pot's neck often featured complicated designs. The Zuni also made bowls for mixing cornmeal and other foods. These were different, however, from the bowls used in rituals. The ritual bowls were painted inside and out, often with water creatures such as dragonflies, frogs, and a serpent named Kolowisi, a hero in many Zuni stories. The Zuni still make pottery today.

Shades of white, black, and brown are commonly used to decorate Zuni pots.

Zuni pottery

Shalako is the most important Zuni religious ceremony. It is a time for giving thanks and paying respects to the spirit world.

Zuni Beliefs

Zuni religion is complicated. But it is possible to begin to understand what the Zuni believe by looking at how they practice their faith. The Zuni see all things as being sacred, from storms to maize. Prayer and rituals keep their lives in balance. Many Zuni today feel that their religion allowed them to stay together as a people, while some other Native American groups broke up or died out.

 The Shalako ceremony takes place every November or December.

Sacred Salt

Every year, Zunis make a **pilgrimage** of about 60 miles (100 km) to Zuni Salt Lake. At the sacred lake, they collect salt for their food and religious ceremonies. The Zuni give thanks to the Salt Mother for her gift. The pilgrimage is an important event in the life of the Zuni and other Pueblo peoples. Roads lead from each village to the lake.

Zuni Salt Lake is very shallow. During the wet season, it is only 4 feet (1.2 m) deep.

The Zuni believe the Salt Mother lives at Zuni Salt Lake.

A Zuni farmer works the soil. The Zuni believe in more than 200 kachina spirits, including ones that help corn ripen.

The Kachina

Every four years, the Zuni make a pilgrimage to the Kachina Village near Flagstaff, Arizona. A **kachina** is the living spirit form of a certain thing in the world. A mesa has its own kachina. So does squash, rain, and an important ancestor. Showing respect to a kachina might allow a person to influence the spirit. For example, the Zuni sometimes call on a kachina to bring rain or heal the sick.

Masks With Spirit Faces

The Zuni believe that long ago the kachina spirits visited the villages. The spirits taught them to make sacred masks that looked like the spirits. Today, each adult male must have a mask made for him by the members of his kiva. He cannot sell it, nor should he buy one. When he dies, his mask is buried with him. That way, his spirit can return for ceremonies.

The Zuni create certain masks from the wood of trees struck by lightning. They believe the wood absorbs the lightning's power.

Kokopelli

The god Kokopelli appears on rock carvings and elsewhere as a humpbacked flute player. In the Zuni religion, Kokopelli oversees the growing of crops and the ability of women to give birth. Some stories say that he carries both seeds and babies on his back.

The Zuni believe Kokopelli brought rain to the Southwest.

Kokopelli brings on spring by playing his flute, and he can create a good harvest. Because of his power over childbearing, he is also part of the Zuni marriage ceremony.

Dancers and Dolls

The masked kachina dancer is a spectacular sight. In full costume, he resembles a bird as big as 10 feet (3 m) tall. The dancer appears to be a supernatural being. For Zuni believers, his presence makes the invisible world of the spirits visible. Today, the Zuni allow outsiders to watch some kachina dances. Other sacred dance ceremonies take place in private.

Timeline of Zuni History

1100s
Ancient peoples leave their towns for unknown reasons.

1539
The Zuni meet the Spanish.

Kachina Dolls

Zuni men create kachina dolls in the shapes of spirits. These dolls, however, are not for play. Fathers, grandfathers, and uncles use the dolls to teach Zuni children about the kachina spirits and religious life. When the children become adults, they might pass on the dolls to their children. Zuni artists, unlike other Pueblo craftspeople, do not usually sell kachina dolls to outsiders.

1680
The Zuni revolt against the Spanish.

1877
Zuni Reservation is founded.

Dancing and singing play a part in many Zuni ceremonies.

Traditional dances and activities are ways for young Zuni to maintain ties to the past and celebrate their culture.

CHAPTER 5

The Zuni Today

Unlike other native peoples, the Zuni were never forced off their lands by soldiers and settlers. Starting in the late 1800s, the U.S. government set aside the land the Zuni were living on as a reservation. In the mid-1900s, the Zuni started to link to the non-Zuni world. Zuni leaders used U.S. government money to provide electricity, water, paved streets, schools, and other services.

In school, children learn the Zuni language. At home, they grow crops in the walled gardens used for centuries by their ancestors.

Today, many Zuni struggle with serious health problems. Others cannot find regular jobs. Young Zuni leave the reservation to find work. But not all the news is bad. About 10,000 live on the 659-square-mile (1,707 sq km) Zuni Reservation in New Mexico. Many still farm. About 8 in 10 households earn money making jewelry, pottery, and animal sculptures. Religious ceremonies are regularly held on the reservation. The Zuni, as always, journey into the future while maintaining close ties with their past. ★

The Zuni once considered pottery making to be a female activity. Today, both men and women take part in this craft.

True Statistics

Number of languages related to Zuni: 0

Height of tallest buildings at Chaco Canyon: 5 stories

Number of Zuni Coronado encountered: About 3,000

Height of Corn Mountain: 500 ft. (150 m)

Years the Zuni spent on Corn Mountain: 12

Number of Zuni villages in the mid-1600s: 3

Number of Zuni towns after 1692: 1

Diameter of a large kiva: More than 60 ft. (18 m)

Maximum height of a kachina dancer: 10 ft. (3 m)

Number of Zuni who served in World War II: More than 200

Size of Zuni Reservation: 659 sq. mi. (1,707 sq km)

Did you find the truth?

(T) The Zuni used rock carvings to help guide them to water.

(F) The Zuni did not participate in the Pueblo Revolt of 1680.

Resources

Books

Bishop, Amanda, and Bobbie Kalman. *Life in a Pueblo*. New York: Crabtree, 2003.

Hicks, Terry Allan. *The Zuni*. New York: Benchmark, 2009.

Lourie, Peter. *The Lost World of the Anasazi*. Honesdale, PA: Boyds Mills, 2007.

Petersen, David. *Chaco Culture National Park*. New York: Children's Press, 1999.

Press, Petra. *The Zuni*. Minneapolis: Compass Point, 2002.

St. Lawrence, Genevieve. *The Pueblo and Their History*. Minneapolis: Compass Point, 2005.

Organizations and Web Sites

Kennedy Museum of Art at Ohio University

www.ohio.edu/museum/zuni

Study a collection of Zuni artworks, including jewelry and carvings.

National History Museum of Los Angeles County

www.nhm.org/site/explore-exhibits/permanent-exhibits/zuni-fetishes

Get a close-up look at Zuni carvings of animals and other figures.

National Museum of the American Indian

www.nmai.si.edu

See exhibits on the lives and culture of Native Americans.

Places to Visit

A:shiwi A:wan Museum and Heritage Center

02E Ojo Caliente Road
Zuni, NM 87327
(505) 782-4403
www.ashiwi-museum.org
Explore Zuni art and culture, and listen to Zunis talk about their lives at this museum on the Zuni Reservation.

Pueblo of Zuni

1203B State Highway 53
Zuni, NM 87327
(505) 782-7000
www.ashiwi.org
Walk the streets of the Zuni village and visit a church painted with kachina figures.

Important Words

adobe (uh-DOH-bee)—dried bricks made of clay, sand, water, and straw

archaeology (AR-kee-OL-uh-jee)—the study of past times and peoples through objects and remains of the past

artifacts (ART-uh-faktz)—objects from a past time

drought (DROUT)—a long period of unusually low rainfall

irrigate (IHR-uh-GATE)—watering crops with saved water

kachina (ka-CHEEN-a)—a wooden doll that represents a god or a spirit of an ancestor, or the spirit itself

kivas (KEE-vuhz)—underground rooms built by Pueblo peoples where important ceremonies or gatherings take place

mesa (MAY-suh)—a broad, flat-topped hill with steep sides

mythical (MITH-i-kuhl)—having to do with traditional stories and beliefs shared by a group of people

pilgrimage (PIL-gruhm-ij)—a journey to a sacred place

reservation (rez-ur-VAY-shuhn)—land set aside for use by Native Americans

rituals (RICH-oo-ulz)—religious ceremonies with specific rules

sacred (SAY-krid)—having to do with religion or something holy

traditions (truh-DISH-uhnz)—patterns of thought or action passed down from generation to generation

Index

Page numbers in **bold** indicate illustrations

About the Authors

Kevin Cunningham has written more than 40 books on disasters, the history of disease, Native Americans, and other topics. Cunningham lives near Chicago with his wife and young daughter.

Peter Benoit is educated as a mathematician but has many other interests. He has taught and tutored high school and college students for many years, mostly in math and science. He also runs summer workshops for writers and students of literature. Benoit has written more than 2,000 poems. His life has been one committed to learning. He lives in Greenwich, New York.

PHOTOGRAPHS © 2011: Alamy Images: 18 (19th era), 15 (Danita Delimont), 10 (John Mitchell), 32 (North Wind Picture Archives), 4, 40 (Chuck Place), 23 (Chris Selby), 8, 35, 42 (Scott Warren/Aurora Photos), 20 (H. Mark Weidman Photography); AP Images: 19 (John A. Bowersmith/Gallup Independent), 28, 29 background (North Wind Picture Archives), cover (Pat Vasquez-Cunningham); Art Resource, NY/Bildarchiv Preussuscher Kulturbesitz: 5 top, 9; Bridgeman Art Library International Ltd., London/New York: 16 (Bibliotheque des Arts Decoratifs, Paris/Archives Charmet), 5 bottom, 31 (Cincinnati Art Museum, Ohio/Gift of the Women's Art Museum Association), 13 (Graham Coton/Private Collection/©Look and Learn), 39 left (Maynard Dixon/Private Collection/Peter Newark American Pictures); Clifford Oliver Photography/www.cliffordoliverphotography.com: 48 bottom; Denver Public Library, Western History Collection/X-30905: 30; Elizabeth Hart: 48 top; Getty Images/Marilyn Angel Wynn/Nativestock.com: 17; iStockphoto: 29 center (Maximilian Allen), 12, 38 left (Daniel Fiverson), 27 (paterne); Kansas State Historical Society, Topeka, Kansas/KansasMemory.org/550: 14; Library of Congress/Edward S. Curtis: 43; National Geographic Stock/W. Langdon Kihn: 22; Nativestock.com/Marilyn "Angel" Wynn: 39 right; NEWSCOM: 34 (Jim Wark/Lonely Planet Images), 37 (Angel Wynn/DanitaDelimont.com); North Wind Picture Archives: 26, 29 bottom; Scholastic Library Publishing, Inc.: 44; ShutterStock, Inc.: back cover (J. Hindman), 36 (Jhaz Photography), 29 top (Pack-Shot); Superstock, Inc./Robert Harding Picture Library: 25; The Art Archive/Picture Desk/W. Langdon Kihn/NGS Image Collection: 38 right; The Design Lab: 6; The Granger Collection, New York: 24 (Timothy O'Sullivan), 3.